Each of the following very real people are brave.

They do incredible things each and every day.

They use their talents to do truly otherworldy feats, sometimes from very far away.

Including the man or woman who stands at this podium, speaking for our country and leading the whole world.

Do you know what else they ALL do?
They also pee and poo!

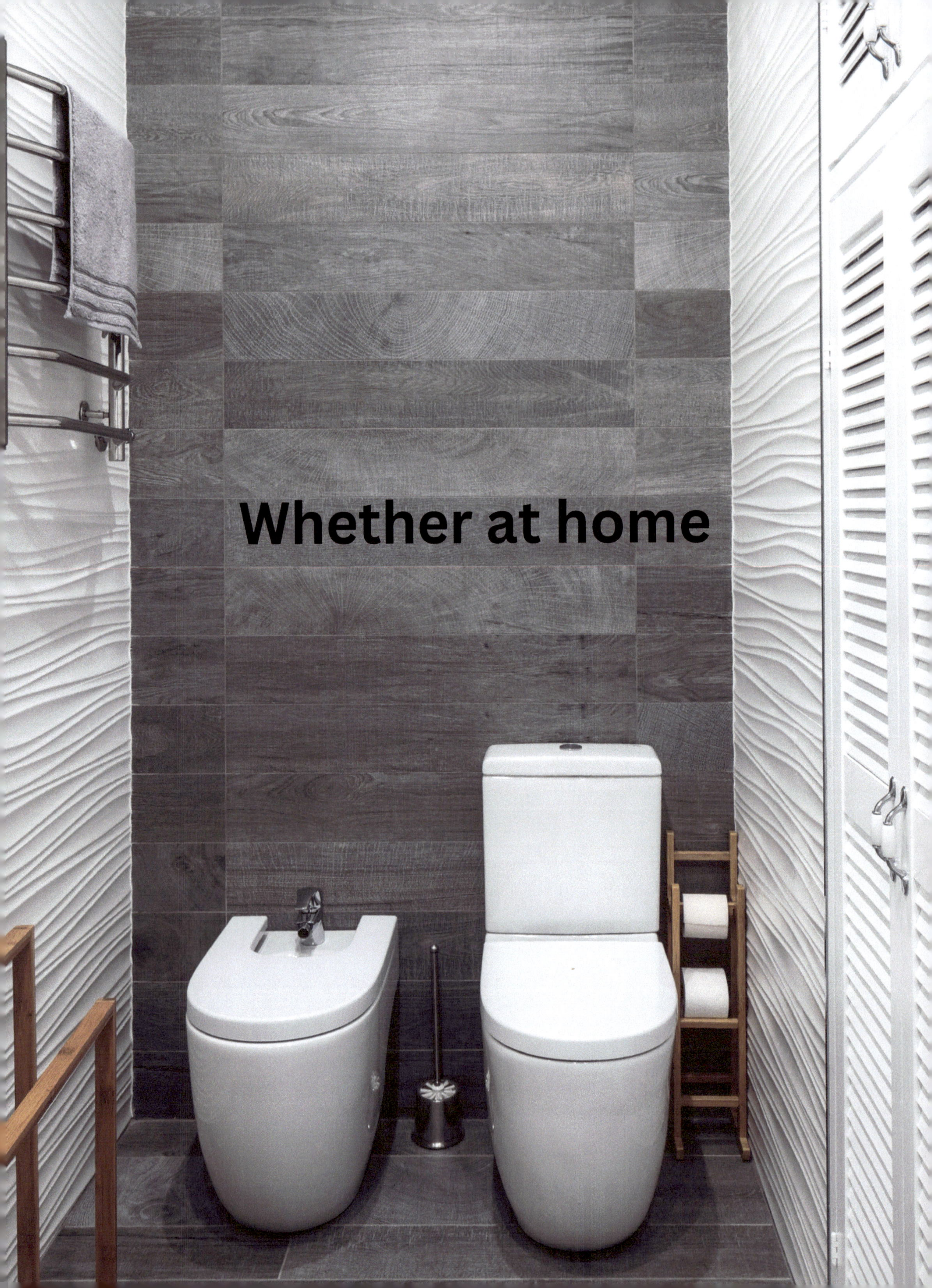

Whether at home

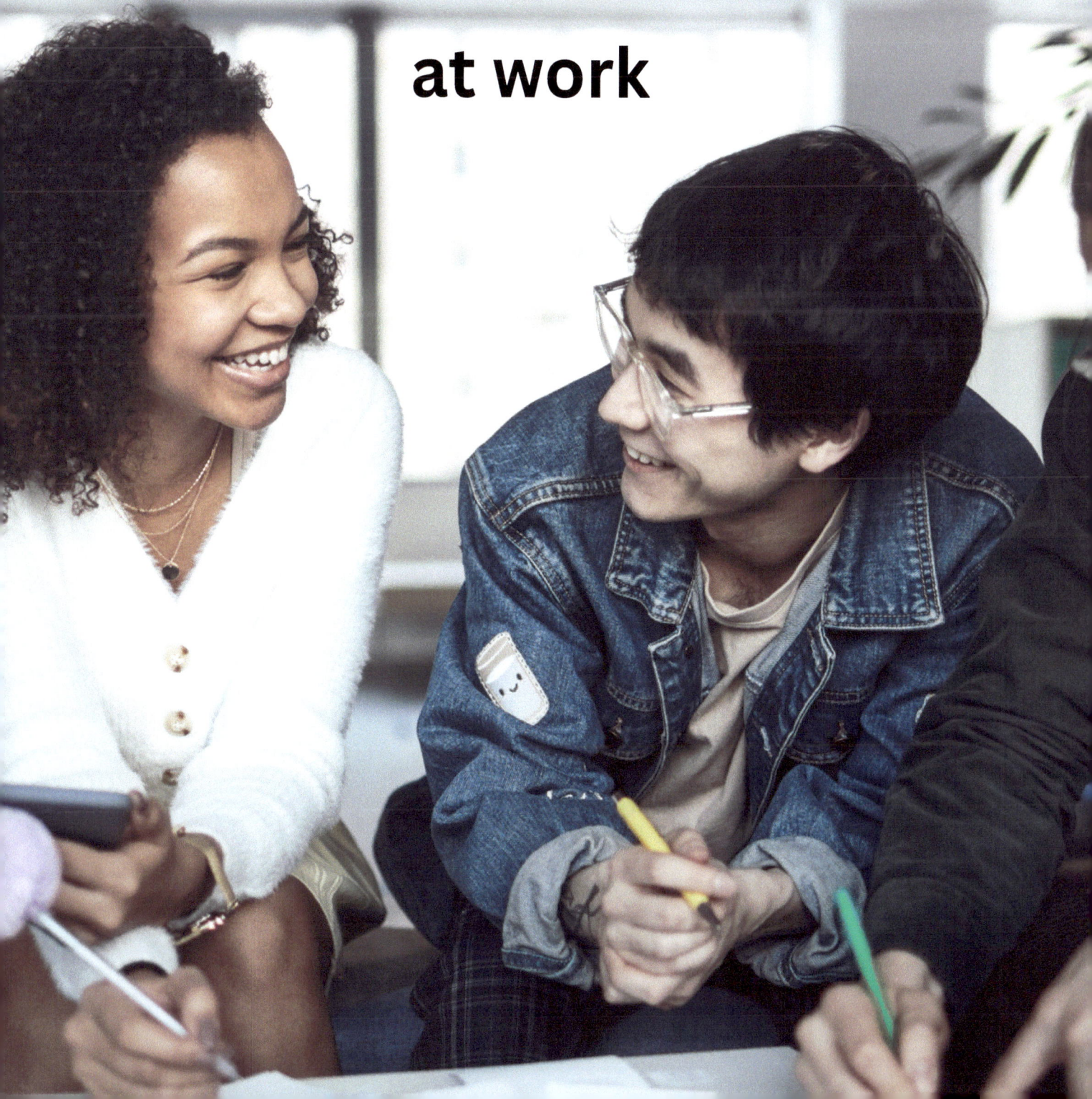

at work

or at preschool

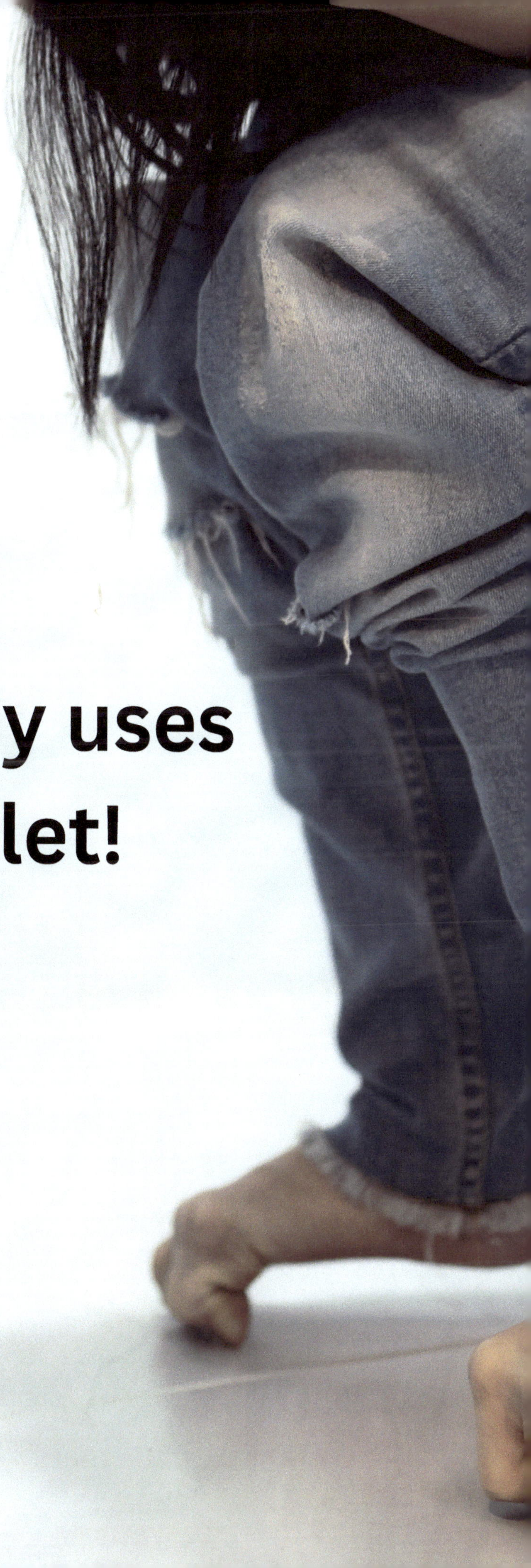

everybody uses
the toilet!

Some use
potty chairs.

Others go with help on the toilet.

Michael makes sure to flush when he's finished.

**Leo soaps up while singing
happy birthday to
his mommy.**

Ellie washes her hands with her friends.

and her teacher gets one paper towel to remind Ellie to use only what she truly needs.

Learning how to use the potty can feel overwhelming. That's okay.

That's why we practice.

Olivia likes to practice by having teddy model how she sits on the toilet.

Aiden counts out five sheets while he waits for his poop to appear.

Mathilde takes her dolly along for the trip.

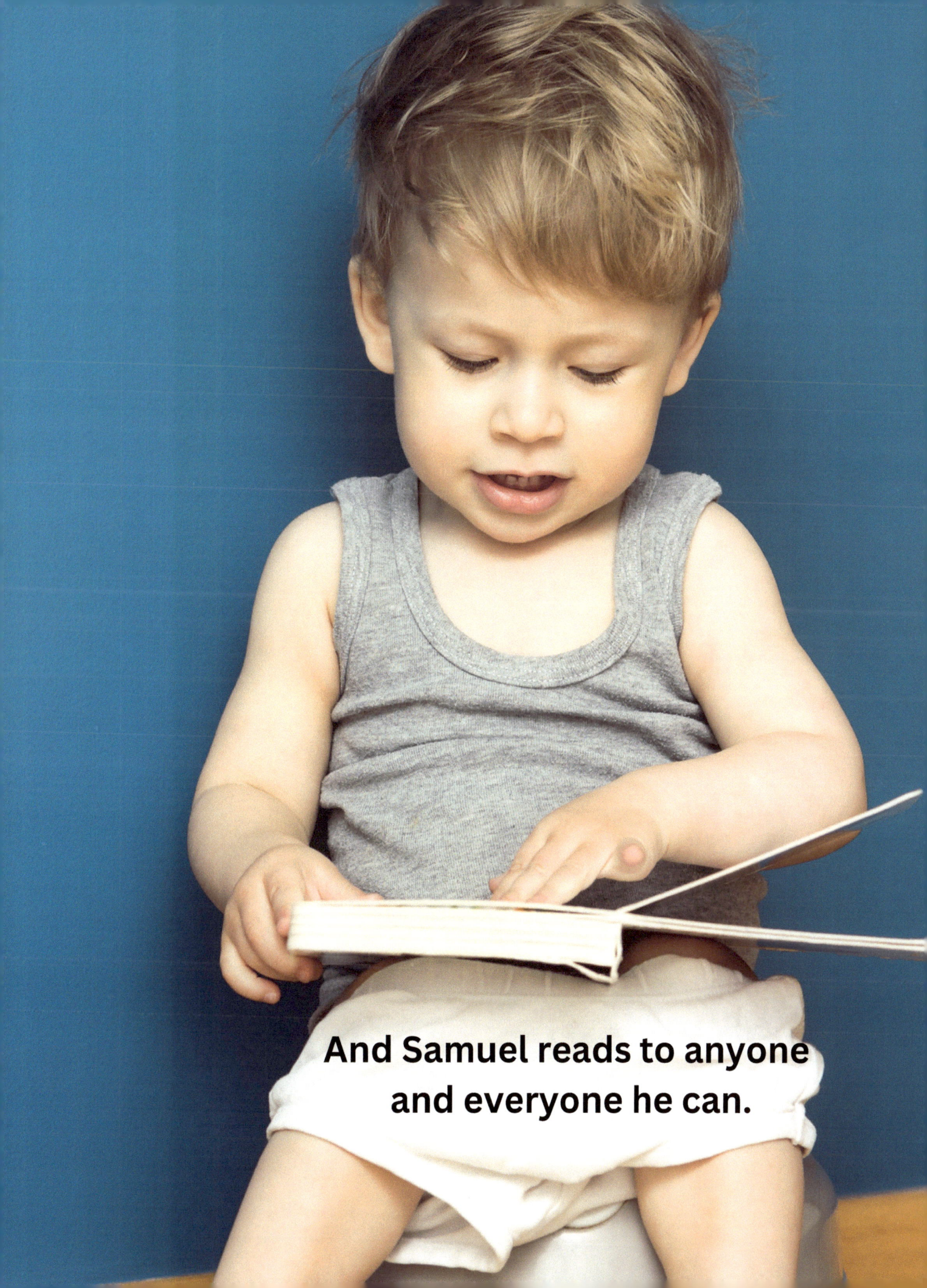

And Samuel reads to anyone
and everyone he can.

Remember, EVERYONE uses the toilet.

And each and
every person
had to learn, just
like you!

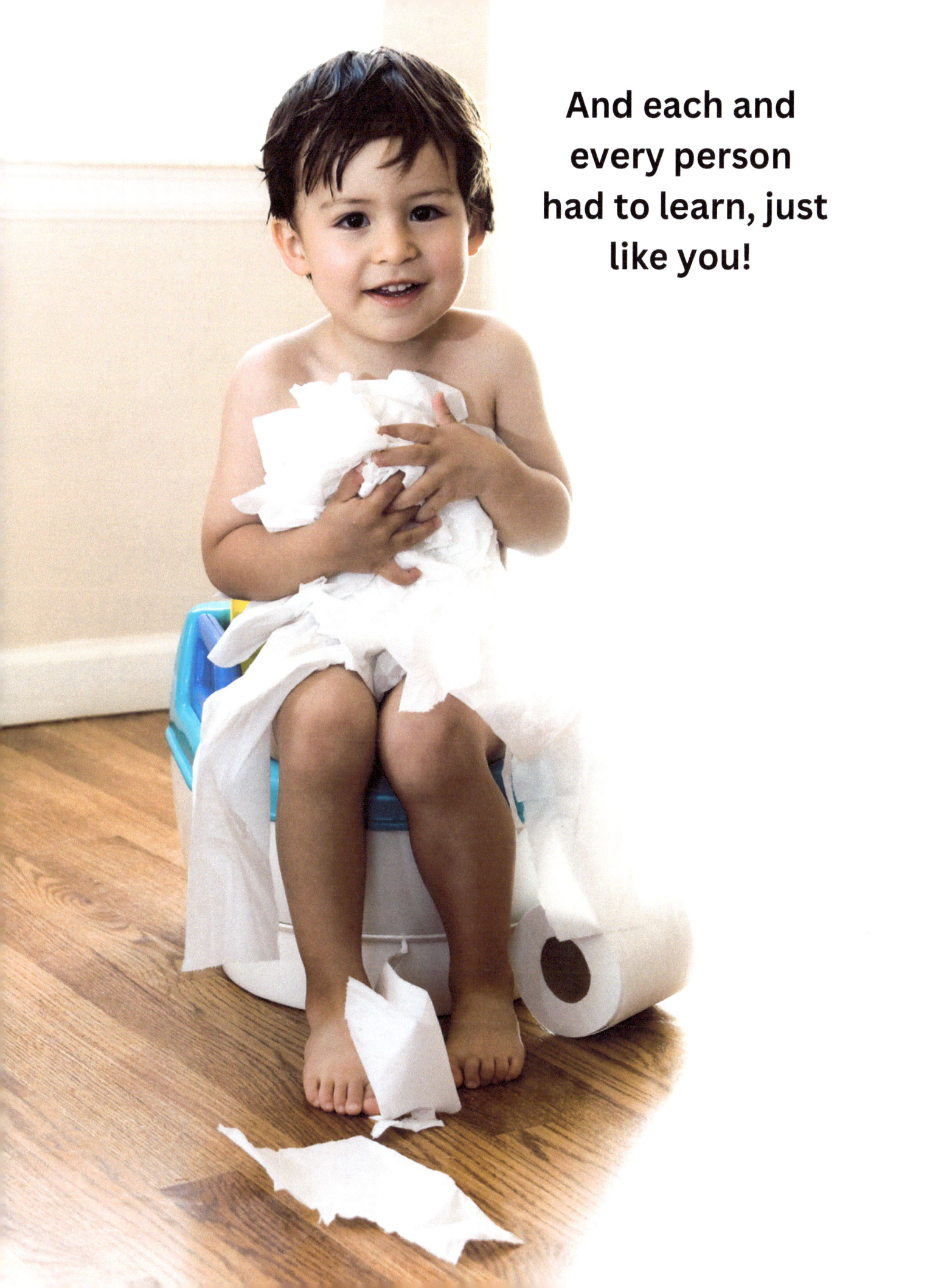

This eBook is dedicated to a boy named Nolan and to every child who likes to see real people doing real things.

Jessica Freilich is the author of "See Yourself Go!" It is her first book. She founded THE POTTY NANNY, an Oh Crap! certified potty training consultancy for parents and the whole child, bringing together her years of truly varied experience working with children. She lives in Charlotte, North Carolina.

To find out more about Jessica, please visit www.the-potty-nanny.com

www.ingramcontent.com/pod-product-compliance
Lightning Source LLC
Chambersburg PA
CBHW042113040426
42448CB00002B/257